IMAGES
of America

KEUKA LAKE

This 1960s aerial photograph of Keuka Lake was taken from the north.

IMAGES
of America

KEUKA LAKE

Charles R. Mitchell

ARCADIA
PUBLISHING

Published by Arcadia Publishing
Charleston, South Carolina

For all general information contact Arcadia Publishing at:
Telephone 843-853-2070
Fax 843-853-0044
E-mail sales@arcadiapublishing.com
For customer service and orders:
Toll-Free 1-888-313-2665

Visit us on the Internet at www.arcadiapublishing.com

Keuka Lake and the bluff are shown in a photograph taken from the east.

CONTENTS

Pt. Comfort

Esperanza

Riley's

Coryell's

Abbots

Dave Ross's Pt.

Pulteney Landing

Gibson's

White Top

Urbana

Two Mile Point

Snug Harbor

Keuka
Lake

Strubble's

Electric Park

Alley's Inn

Branchport

Keuka
College

Hammondsport

Penn Yan

Empire State Winery
&

Willow Grove

Finton's

Crosby

Camp Arey

Ogo-wa-go

Sturdevants's

Keuka

Care Naught

Grove Springs

The Elms

Corning

Davie's Landing

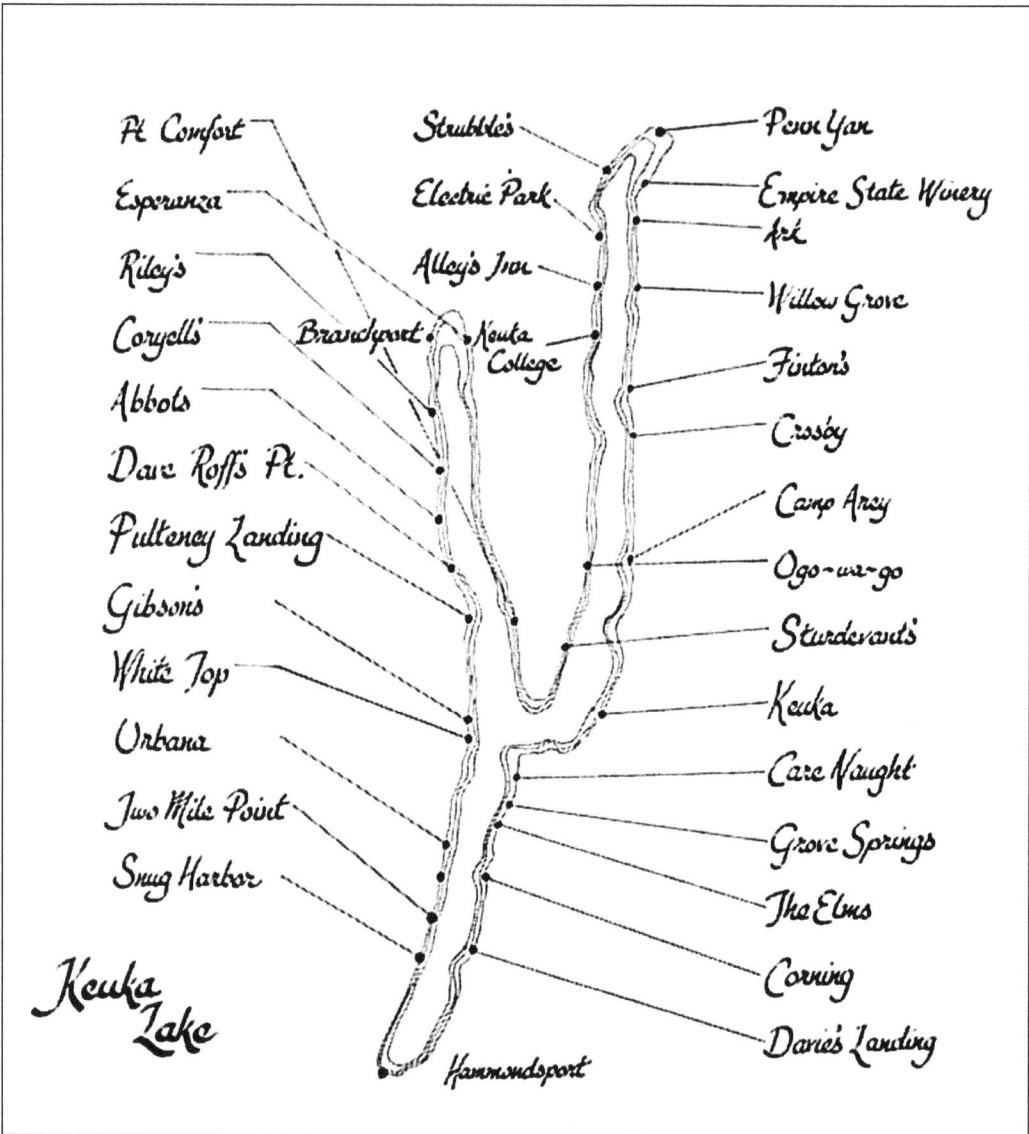

Many of the photographic subjects featured in this book can be found on this map of steamboat landings.

INTRODUCTION

In Native American legend, the Creator, or Great Spirit, looked with special favor upon what is now western New York State and placed his hand on the land to bless it. The imprint of his hand formed the Finger Lakes. Geologists tell us that the valleys were formed by the glaciers as they moved south, leaving rubble or drumlins at the ends. When the glaciers withdrew, the melting ice filled the dammed-up valleys, creating lakes larger than they are today. Now the 11 lakes are from 3 to 40 miles in length and from 30 to 632 feet in depth. Keuka is more than 19 miles long, with 59 miles of shoreline and a depth of 187 feet.

In the Seneca language, *Keuka* means "lake with an elbow," or "canoe landing place." It was called Crooked Lake by the white settlers. In 1857, Keuka became the official name, to bring the lake's name into conformity with the Native American names of the other Finger Lakes. Today, the name Crooked Lake has been adopted by some businesses.

Collecting photographs to tell the story of Keuka Lake is difficult only in that there are too many to choose from. *Keuka Lake Revisited* follows *Penn Yan and Keuka Lake* and *Hammondsport and Keuka Lake,* all showing images of the lake, the area around it, and the people who lived there. Many more beautiful images are available, but the number that can be used here is limited.

As a photographer, I have again selected the images first and have then written captions to accompany them. Because I have arranged them in chapters to tell a story, I run the risk of writing an incomplete history. Having made that apology, I trust that the history is accurate. Whenever possible, original photographs are used; many I printed from the original negatives or glass plates.

If the images are borrowed from individuals, they are so acknowledged in the captions that accompany the photographs. Some of the images are from the collection of my business, the Photographic Center. Many of the postcard images are from the collection of Ralph Wilkes, for which I am grateful. The majority of the photographs come from the Oliver House Museum in Penn Yan. Within the general collection there are three important collections that are used here: the Rapalee-Vosberg glass plates are used for the cover as well as most of the photographs of Central Point; the images of the Amsbury Collection (reproduced from four- by five-inch glass plates) show life in the 1890s around Penn Yan and the north end of the lake; the images from the second half of the 20th century are the newspaper photographs of Dick Eisenhart. A reporter, he recently donated his photographs to the museum.

I am indebted to some people for the help they have given me in producing this book. In addition to the sources of the images acknowledged above, I have received much research help and encouragement from Idele Dillon, director of the Oliver House Museum. As with my other two Keuka Lake books, the accuracy of the text is due to the sharp-eyed Elliott Vorce's proofreading and to the technical expertise of my wife, Melissa.

One

THE LAKE

Many areas of the world have a special place in the hearts of the people who have lived there. Keuka Lake is no exception and is loved by thousands who reside there or return on an annual basis. Many others would live there if they could but do come back when they retire. The natural beauty adds considerably to the quality of life to be found around Keuka Lake.

Keuka is 715 feet above sea level, has 59 miles of shoreline, and is 187 feet deep at its deepest point. The bluff that forms Keuka Lake's Y shape is its most prominent feature. Rising 800 feet above Keuka's waters at the southern end, it tapers down to the point of being very shallow at the north end. At one time, the bluff was an island. The east branch—with Penn Yan at the north end—is approximately 12 miles long; the west branch—with Branchport at the north end—is about 8 miles long. Penn Yan and Branchport are 8 miles apart. The main branch, with Hammondsport at the southern end, is 7 miles long. The average width is approximately a mile, with the widest point at the end of the bluff at more than 2 miles.

There are numerous photographs of Keuka Lake and the bluff dating back to the 1850s, when the earliest cameras came into the area. The drawing above is from that same era. The broad hillside just north of the Grove Springs area would appear to be the artist's vantage point, as it is the only place on the lake where you can see the ends of both branches. Most of the hillsides were planted in vineyards at that time.

The absence of a highway on the east side of the lake and the lack of steamboats in this aerial photograph date it to the late 1920s or early 1930s. Skyline Drive stands out prominently down the middle of the bluff. In the hot, dry summer of 1855, most of the woods on the bluff burned. As the story goes, the conflagration drove the rattlesnakes into the lake, where they then drowned.

This more modern view from the Wagener Mansion front lawn looks to the south toward Hammondsport, which is at the end of the main branch of Keuka Lake. The 1833 mansion was one of the homes built by Abraham Wagener, an early settler and one of the founders of Penn Yan. The house, now a private home not open to the public, is highly visible from almost anywhere around the southern half of the lake.

The east branch of Keuka Lake and Waneta Lake can be seen in this *c.* 1920 view made from the original glass plate. The lawn at the Wagener Mansion on the bluff was a great vantage point from which to view the lake. Today, trees obscure the view to the east.

On top of the Wagener Mansion is a widow's walk, which offers an even more spectacular view than that seen from the front lawn. This vantage point allows one to see the road coming more than 800 vertical feet up the face of the bluff, past the Garrett Chapel on the left, to the top.

The front porch of the Wagener Mansion, as well as the view from the end of the bluff, can be seen here. This 1950s photograph shows the house when it was open to the public.

The commanding view of the main branch of the lake, Lakes Lamoka and Waneta, and the surrounding countryside made this a favored scenic view.

Shocks of corn are rarely seen today but were common when this photograph overlooking Keuka Lake was taken in the 1940s. The view is to the west, and the bluff is on the right. This field and most like it are now vineyards.

Above Keuka's east side is Lake Waneta, a small lake connected to Lake Lamoka. These small lakes are not Finger Lakes but do provide great fishing. A Native American village set between Lamoka and Waneta spawned the legend of ill-fated lovers from opposing tribes who chose to drown rather than be separated. The lakes' names are their legacy.

In this 1950s photograph of the bluff, taken from the east side on Silsbee Road, Penn Yan appears in the distance at the end of the east branch on the right. This view of Keuka Lake provides a breathtaking scene any time of the year.

The scenery around Keuka Lake has long drawn artists who usually find their favorite view, as with the artist shown here on Bully Hill. The Y shape of the lake, the vineyards, and the steep hillsides are especially attractive to artists, including photographers. Working in all media, the many artists around the lake provide a wide variety of art.

Sitting at the end of the dock looking at the lake is a great way to spend time. The panoramic view, as well as the gentle movement of the clouds and water, can be very relaxing.

Most mornings on Keuka Lake are this quiet, the lake as smooth as glass. Looking from the west side at the bluff, this view shows the Wagener Mansion at the top left.

Burnell Studios in Penn Yan produced this very popular view of Keuka Lake from the east, with the bluff on the right. This photograph and many other of William Burnell's lake scenes, often hand-tinted and framed, are commonly found hanging in homes and businesses.

One of the best views of Keuka Lake is from Silsbee Road above the Grove Springs area. The vineyards have been replaced by houses, but the view is otherwise unchanged and still spectacular. By moving just a few hundred feet along the road, one can see both Branchport at the end of the west branch and Penn Yan at the end of the east branch.

17

Another spectacular view of Keuka Lake can be found on the road above the house Esperanza, looking down the west branch. With vineyards in the foreground and the steep drop to the lake, this view is unmatched anywhere in the Finger Lakes. Local residents like to bring first-time visitors here but make them close their eyes until they reach the top of the hill; then they look back.

John N. Rose and his family came to the Finger Lakes from Virginia with their slaves and built a number of homes, including the house above, in 1838, which he named Esperanza. The local Native Americans assisted by bringing sand in their canoes. When the house was completed, he freed his slaves. Ironically, the mansion is rumored to have been a stop on the Underground Railroad.

This elegant photograph was taken behind Esperanza c. 1900. The tract that the Roses developed contained 1,050 acres, all east of the west branch of Keuka Lake. Esperanza overlooked another Rose home called Chestnuts, which the state razed for a park. Esperanza had numerous uses in the 20th century: a private home, the county poorhouse, a winery, and lastly an inn. It is once again an inn.

Orchards are not as common as vineyards along Keuka Lake. When the trees blossom in the spring, however, they are breathtaking, even in black and white, as this photograph illustrates.

The Garrett Chapel was built by the Garrett family of winemakers 700 feet above Keuka on a steep hillside. It was dedicated in 1931 as a memorial to the Garretts' son, who had died of tuberculosis. The chapel is a family burial place, as a crypt in the chapel contains the family remains. Designs throughout the crypt depict the idealism of young manhood. Windows in the chapel contain various scenes from the life of Christ.

20

A photograph that shows the entire Garrett Chapel and the lake is rare; today trees obscure both. This view was apparently taken in the early 1930s, when the chapel was new. Its end-of-the-bluff location does not diminish the popularity of the chapel as a tourist destination.

The arches on the east side of the Garrett Chapel are one of its most photogenic features. This postcard view dates from the 1930s. The arches remain just as beautiful today, but maintaining the view requires periodic pruning of the trees.

"Willow Bank," as this photograph is titled, was probably taken at a family gathering, most likely on the Fourth of July. The people have dressed in their finest, artfully displaying their boats. W.J. Harris took this photograph from his floating photography studio c. 1900. The barge provided a steady platform that he used for scenes of the shore as well as boats on the lake.

The vineyards on the steep hills on the west side of Keuka provide a view of the bluff and the east side. In comparison to the photograph on the top of page 98, the end of the bluff bears no vineyards today. Hillsides near the lake are less steep and easier to work.

Following an ancient Seneca Indian custom of circling the lake with fires in thanks for a successful harvest, tribe members returned each year until 1917 to celebrate with this ceremony. Today, the Labor Day weekend lighting of flares around the lake continues that tradition.

The bay on the left is known as Brandy Bay because of the distillery that was once there. Grapes were not easily transported long distances, but brandy was; it was more compact, did not spoil, and had higher value. Keuka College's Ball Hall is the building visible in the distance.

The little Trout Fisher - Penn Yan, N.Y. who caught Trout with his Nose."

Harry Morse and his trout are local legends and made for a bestselling postcard. Seven-year-old Harry and his mother were in a rowboat on Brandy Bay one Sunday in 1873 when he looked over the side into the water. An eight-pound trout apparently mistook his nose for something to eat and bit on it. The combination of the trout's hit and Harry's involuntary drawing-back flipped the trout into the boat. His mother, hearing his scream, turned to see her son's bloody face and a trout floundering in the bottom of the boat. She used an oar to subdue it. A steamboat captain in his adult life, Harry still carried the scar on his nose.

Electric Park was so named because it was adjacent to the electric supply for the trolley. The park spanned two acres and included public docks, refreshments, picnic facilities, and a dance pavilion. Its main attraction was the use of outdoor electric lights. No liquor was allowed because Keuka College was only half a mile away.

This area, named after the owner of the land on the right, was called Hanford Cove. Today, this Penn Yan village park is known as Indian Pines. The formally dressed gentlemen in the rowboats are probably going fishing.

Family gatherings at the lake, especially on holidays, have always been popular. The small cottage named Tree Tops would have made for crowded accommodations on this Fourth of July weekend. This crowd, with their "proper" clothing, managed to avoid sunburn. We should consider ourselves fortunate that we do not need to dress as formally at the lake now.

The Branchport end of the lake tends to be quite shallow and marshy. This photograph, taken late in the day, shows many fishing boats probably after trout. They may have been preparing to fish at night; lights, hung over the side of their boats, attracted bait, which then attracted larger fish.

26

Fishing for sport or relaxation is a major activity on the lake. In the early 1900s, fishing occurred from the dock, as seen in this photograph produced from a glass plate; today, fishing from motorboats is more prevalent. Rainbow, lake, and brown trout have always been plentiful, as well as both large- and small-mouth bass, pickerel, and land-locked salmon.

Allie and Will Stone show off a fantastic day's catch. These 56 trout, weighing a total of 164 pounds, were caught on a Seth Green rig. The Lake Keuka Navigation Company advertised, "Other catches almost as large are being made daily. Lake Keuka is rapidly becoming the finest Fishing Resort in the state. It is already the favorite Vacation Resort."

The people and boats shown in this postcard view of Central Point would appear to be using a public beach; however, the point was private. This collection of period cottages comprised a community, with people staying for the summer and not just the weekends, as is now often the case.

Mildred Rapalee helps to show off this string of eight fish. She always seemed to be available to pose with fish that someone in the family had caught that morning. She also must have enjoyed dressing up; her costumes are usually interesting.

28

Again, Mildred Rapalee is pictured with a fish, although she was not the only one to be photographed "holding" this large lake trout. Glass plate negatives document other family members in similar Central Point scenes.

This print of Central Point was made from a glass plate negative from the Rapalee-Vosberg Collection. Many of the cottages on Central Point today appear virtually unchanged from this photograph. A sign is still attached to a tree in front of one of the cottages where this landing used to be.

This photograph, made from the original glass plate, shows the family gathered to admire the day's trout catch. It was taken from the Rapalee-Vosberg Collection at the Oliver House Museum in Penn Yan. This collection of images taken at the family cottage at Central Point on Keuka's east side is an important part of the museum's photography archive.

The docks today are not as high as the one shown here on Central Point. The height was necessary to accommodate the steamboats that stopped here to deliver supplies or board passengers. Although the steamers had regularly scheduled stops, they would stop at private docks when signaled in by a white flag.

All of Keuka's beauty is not reserved for the summer. The picnic tables at Keuka Lake State Park, located at the north end of the west branch, are the setting for this beautiful winter scene.

Not too many years ago, there were only a few Canada geese that declined to take the flight north and spent the winter on the lake. Now hundreds, if not thousands, winter-over on Keuka Lake. Many are year-round residents, to the point of becoming a nuisance.

Camp Arey was started as a science camp by Prof. Albert Arey in 1905. Instruction was given on birds, minerals, trees, wildflowers, insects, and other similar subjects. Athletics were also stressed, with the use of extensive fitness facilities. The camp had its own electricity for lighting, raised its own vegetables, and maintained a dairy for milk.

Camp Arey was reputed to be the first organized summer camp in the United States. At the time of this c. 1930 photograph, it was being operated as a fresh-air camp for girls. Some of the original buildings stand today. A portion of the property is currently a trailer park.

Camp Arey, located on Eggleston's Point on the east branch across from the end of the bluff, was at one time owned by John D. Rockefeller. A wheelchair was even stored there for use when he visited, which he never did. Although it is private property today, it was for many years a camp. This 1936 photograph shows a golf class.

Camp Arey had two docks—one for freight and the one shown here for swimming. The water off Eggleston's Point is very deep and must have been excellent for diving. The pilings at the left of the diving platform were used to secure the steamboats.

This postcard view of the Keuka Hotel reflects some artistic license. The houses near the hotel are not shown. More than the "post office" existed across the road, and the road coming down was located farther to the north. Visitors probably neither noticed nor cared.

This *c.* 1920 winter view of the Keuka Hotel shows the sea wall as few people saw it. A beach lined with rowboats would be more familiar. A brochure from the early 1900s stated, "This is the hotel nearest the trout fishing grounds, and every season the house is crowded with enthusiastic fishermen. The place is home-like; the cuisine is unsurpassed. There is no quieter and better conducted place on the lake." A concrete sea wall was added *c.* 1914, eliminating the beach.

The Keuka Hotel was built in 1904, which is the vintage of this stereographic image. In 1912, Bessie Young purchased the hotel and ran it until the late 1960s. An early brochure claimed there were 100 rooms, a figure that must have included nearby cottages rented by the hotel. What an asset that hotel would be today! (Courtesy Don Stork.)

The Keuka Hotel boasted a dance pavilion, which jutted out into the lake perpendicular to the shore. Dance bands were featured. It was claimed that Hoagy Carmichael wrote the words to "Stardust" here while playing in the band. Fred Waring and Rudy Vallee also appeared at the Keuka Hotel. The pavilion was later turned parallel to shore and, as late as the 1950s, was used as a skating rink. A favorite game of the young men was to "crack the whip" in front of one of the openings over the water.

Keuka Village's Switzerland Inn has been a favorite gathering place on the lake for many years. Originally located where the Keuka Hotel was later built, it was moved to the present site in 1894 by Frank Switzer. Over the years, it has been expanded as a bar and restaurant so much that it is now approximately twice the size shown here.

A large hotel like the Grove Springs would have had numerous guests sending cards to friends and relatives all over the country, telling them about Keuka Lake and its great accommodations. Because of this, cards like the one shown here are quite common today.

36

The Grove Springs Hotel on the east side was the largest resort on the lake, having 250 rooms. At the time it was built in 1880, it had all the latest conveniences, including indoor plumbing. The two gazebos on the dock at the right provided shelter for those waiting for steamboats. The hotel burned in 1922, but the house seen on the shore remains.

An unnamed stream runs into Keuka Lake, forming the point in front of the Grove Springs Hotel. The walk along the beach, along with the rustic bridge crossing that stream, was called "Lover's Lane." This Harris photograph shows lovers in a rowboat under that bridge.

37

The Hotel Lakeside looks far better than this today. The structure remains unchanged, but extensive decks have been added to provide some of the most delightful outdoor dining available on Keuka Lake. In the summer, as many diners arrive by boat as by car.

Gibson's Grocery Store was part of the complex at Gibson's Landing on West Lake Road across from the end of the bluff. In the 1960s, the store was relocated across the road but later closed. The structure at the extreme left of the photograph was originally a bus stop shelter.

The Gibson House on Keuka's west side held 65 rooms, according to one publication, but this may have included rooms in nearby houses that were rented by the same owners. In the 1920s, the decision to locate a paved state highway either on the west or east side of the lake was to be made by the governor after visiting Keuka. Most of the farmers on the west side chose that day to drive their wagons past the Gibson House repeatedly, causing a very dusty picnic. The governor decided the west side needed the highway.

The Holmes Inn was located on West Lake Road between the Penn Yan Municipal Water Plant and Brandy Bay. It was a small inn well known for its food. The structure is still there today; however, it has been remodeled, expanded, and renamed the Colonial Motel.

LAKE KEUKA

THE FALLS
EGGELLSTONS
GLEN

Prior to Camp Arey, a concession stand at Eggleston's Point had picnic tables and sold ice cream. People would hike through the glen to the falls, which are 110 feet high and flow into a gorge that in places is 200 feet deep. An early advertisement for the Grove Springs Hotel stated that stagecoaches left the hotel every afternoon at 1:00 p.m. for Eggleston's Falls.

Alley's Inn was built as the Lakeside Hotel. Later, after a few years as a sanitarium, it became the home of the Keuka Yacht Club. Meals were served, and often members chose to stay in one of the 19 rooms overnight or for more extended periods. After suffering financial difficulties in 1914, the club was sold to Frank and Maude Alley, who ran it as a very popular lake spot.

At one time, the building on the shore in the center housed the Lakeside Sanitarium, which specialized in surgery, diseases of women, and electrotherapeutics. Under different management and renamed the Keuka Sanitarium, the building had its own yacht to transport patients from various points on the east branch. Alley's Inn was no longer a public place in this 1950s aerial photograph. Additional apartment houses were built, and the inn was razed.

One of the streams that feeds Keuka Lake enters through the village of Hammondsport. In 1935, it changed course and literally ran through the town, causing great damage. Removing the stones and rubble left behind took a long time. The glen east of the village contains this beautiful waterfall, a great place for children to hike and explore.

Two

THE BOATS

Steamboats operated on Keuka Lake from the launching of the *Keuka* in 1835 until the retirement of the *Penn Yan* in 1922. During the peak year of operations in 1895, there were seven steamboats on Keuka Lake. All the boats that were on the lake are pictured in this chapter except the *Keuka I, Keuka II,* and *Steuben I,* for which no photographs are known to exist or which predate photography in this area.

Originally, the steamboats were designed to carry only freight. Grapes, the main cargo, were transported to the railroads at the ends of the lake for shipment to the cities or to the wineries. Later, passengers used the steamers as the only reliable transportation in the area, but freight still had priority. On Sundays, the steamboats operated for passengers only and were filled with those on summer excursions. Prohibition and the faster, more easily accessible automobile were responsible for the end of the steamboat era on Keuka Lake.

Steamboats were not the only craft on the lake; rowboats, sailboats, and powerboats were all built here. In the late 19th and early 20th centuries, numerous nearby rowboat manufacturers existed, and Penn Yan boats were made locally until recently.

The *William L. Halsey* is shown in Penn Yan harbor in January 1892. Viewed under the Liberty Street Bridge is the private yacht *Governor Hill*, renamed the *Earl*. On the right, another boat, shrouded for the winter, can be seen. Boats usually wintered in Hammondsport, which was more likely to be ice-free. The Penn Yan end, being shallow, froze almost every year.

In this W.J. Harris photograph, the *Mary Bell* cruises south near the end of the bluff *c.* 1900. People on the boat have spotted Harris's floating studio and hang out the windows and wave. This image, like many at that time, was made into a postcard.

The *Mary Bell* passes the Elms Point and approaches the Grove Springs Hotel docks *c.* 1900. This beautiful photograph may have been posed while the photographer (probably W.J. Harris) and the people on the point waited for the boat to pass.

The *Holmes* leaves the Hammondsport docks *c.* 1905. This Sunday excursion has passengers coming to Hammondsport on the Erie Railroad and riding the lake on Erie's steamboat (note the Erie diamond on the smokestack). If the travelers did not return to Hammondsport, they rode the New York Central or the Great Northern from Penn Yan to complete their journey.

"Along the Dock, Penn Yan, NY" is the title of this postcard, which shows the *Cricket* tied ahead of either the *Halsey* or the *Holmes* at the railroad docks. The steamers trans-loaded freight to and from the railroad here. The *Cricket* sits at the Guile and Windnagle dock because its competitors controlled the other docks. Once, when the *Cricket* was heavily loaded at the dock, the *Halsey* came into the harbor so fast and with such a high wake that the *Cricket* was swamped.

The *Lulu*, built by A.W. Springstead in Hammondsport in 1878, was 78 feet long with a 30-foot beam. The boat was the namesake of Lulu Mott, who ran a boardinghouse in Hammondsport. It was the only steamboat on Keuka Lake with which a fatality was connected. A deck hand, filling a bucket with water, was pulled into the lake and drowned.

The *Mary Bell* approaches the Keuka Hotel docks in this *c.* 1900 postcard photograph. Built by the Union Dry Docks Company at Hammondsport in 1892, the *Mary Bell* was the largest and grandest of the steamboats. Its launching was said to have drawn a crowd of 10,000 spectators. With two 700-horsepower engines and twin screws, the *Mary Bell* was 164 feet long, had a 24-foot beam, and was rated to carry 650 passengers, although it was not unheard of to squeeze in a few hundred more.

The *Halsey*, the *Holmes*, and the bow of the *West Branch* are shown here on a cold winter day at the railroad dock in Penn Yan. The *William L. Halsey* and the *Farley Holmes* looked identical, both built for the Crooked Lake Navigation Company by A.W. Springstead in Hammondsport. The *Halsey* was actually longer at 130 feet (compared to the *Holmes*'s 120 feet), but they both had the same steam engine with a 30-inch bore and a 6-foot stroke.

47

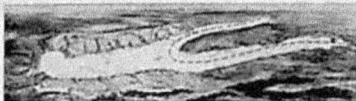

"Around the loop" was a popular summer excursion for local residents, combining a boat and trolley ride. Taking a picnic lunch, going down to the dock at Penn Yan, paying 30¢, and boarding a steamer, one had a day's outing on the lake. Children could be put on the boat for the day. In those less litigious times, mothers knew the crew would take care of the children until the boat docked at Branchport. If the children were fortunate to have received an extra nickel, they could get ice cream while they waited for the trolley for the ride home.

48

The *Cricket* is shown on a summer excursion cruise in the east branch near the end of the bluff. Named for owner Samuel McMath's daughter Crissy, the *Cricket* was the last steamer for public transportation built on Keuka. Operated by the Lee Line and captained by Philo Lee, it was steel-hulled like the *Mary Bell*, but at 82 feet was smaller and therefore often chartered by the college. The *Cricket* burned at the dock in Hammondsport in 1909.

The *Holmes* was renamed the *Yates II* in 1904. The steamer is seen here tied to the dock at Willow Grove on Keuka's east side. This was not a regular freight stop, but as can be seen by the size of the dock, it could only accommodate passengers. The *Yates II* was scrapped in 1915.

The *Mary Bell* was the "Queen" of the lake. Harry Morse, the pilot of the steamer, conceived the idea in 1895 of rafting three boats together for a moonlight excursion, with a band aboard each boat. Gangways joined the boats so that passengers could move between the *Mary Bell*, the *Halsey*, and the *Holmes*. The music and dancing continued until the next morning. The fare was only 25¢.

The *Mary Bell* is pictured here from the stern. A string of electric lights, consisting of 180 colored bulbs, can be seen strung from the stack and rigging. In addition, the boat had electric running lights and searchlights, which were shone on shore at docks and cottages—all unusual in 1900.

The *Urbana*, built by A.W. Springstead at Hammondsport in 1880, was 120 feet long with a 20-foot beam. The steamer is shown here on an excursion. The "running deer" on the walking beam can be seen clearly in this photograph. The *Urbana* was dismantled in 1904.

The *West Branch* was so named because the boat operated primarily from Pulteney to Branchport. Built by A.W. Springstead in 1883 at Hammondsport for the Crooked Lake Navigation Company, it operated until it was dismantled in 1902.

The crew of the *Mary Bell* poses on the upper deck *c.* 1895. The captain was responsible—as on all steamers at that time—for booking freight. The pilot was responsible for navigation and actually running the boat. The rest of the crew fed coal to the boilers, handled freight, or were deck hands.

This picture of the *Penn Yan* at the dock in Hammondsport differs in appearance from the other photographs of the *Penn Yan* or the *Mary Bell*, especially the one on the top of page 50. In an attempt to make the steamboat more efficient, a gasoline engine was installed. This changed the operating characteristics so radically that it was necessary to remove the third deck and move the cabin down. The gas engine vibrated so much it loosened the rivets in the hull. The *Penn Yan* was never the same after its transition.

The *Steuben* (formerly the *Halsey*) sank at the dock in Hammondsport. An elaborate system of beams was placed around the sunken craft, and the boat was gradually winched up while the water was being pumped out. The *Steuben* was successfully righted and put back into service, only to sink again in 1917 in Penn Yan; it was subsequently scrapped.

The *George R. Youngs* was built at Penn Yan in 1864 by Ben Springstead. The boat was 130 feet in length with a 19-foot beam. It had a steam engine with a 30-inch cylinder and a 5-foot stroke. In 1873, the boat was renamed the *Steuben* (the second) and operated until 1879.

In the 1890s, grass from the swampy area on the west side of the outlet came into Penn Yan, causing boat paddle wheels and propellers to fail. To correct this, a wall of planks attached to pilings was built from six to eight feet high. Weeds and sediment stirred up by the passing boats would be carried downstream by the channeled current. The dike was a success, although it did require the boats to travel at lower speeds to prevent damage from their wakes, like the ones that swamped the *Cricket*. The tops of the pilings can still be seen. In the photograph above, a pile driver is installing the pilings to which the board wall was attached. Below, a steamboat is coming out of Penn Yan.

T.O. Hamlin's yacht *Red Jacket* is shown, most likely in front of his East Bluff Drive cottage Heart's Content, in 1908. Hamlin was the secretary-treasurer and eventually the president of the Crooked Lake Navigation Company with William Halsey.

The private steam yacht *Mascot* was rebuilt and fitted with a gasoline engine. It was 65 feet long with a $10^{1}/_{2}$-foot beam. Renamed *Bell*, it joined other private yachts, such as the *Madge*, *Carrie*, and *Arrow*. Races between private boat owners regularly occurred to prove who had the fastest boat on the lake.

The *City of Rochester* or the *City of Elmira* is shown here in a postcard view. These two "tubs" were gasoline powered and were designed for freight, although they did on occasion carry passengers. During storms and high water in the flood of 1935, people feared they would break loose and cause damage. They were beached at Crosby and eventually scrapped.

Penn Yan harbor was always a busy place c. 1895. In addition to the two sailboats, the *Lulu* and the bow of the *Halsey* can be seen on the left. The railroad dock is the long building in the center right. This is one of the few photographs of the *Lulu*.

Murray Wright designed and built the K-boat on Keuka Lake. The K-boat is a wooden sailboat for three to four people, with a single rudder and center movable keel. Many of these boats are still seen locally; Camp Cory, the YMCA camp south of Penn Yan, has its own fleet. The water tower at Keuka College can be seen in the background.

This view shows E-scows racing on a summer day. E-scows are a class of racing boats, flat-bottomed with thin rudders and leeboards rather than keels. The scows head north at the end of the bluff, across from the Keuka Yacht Club. (Courtesy Ed Webber.)

57

Iceboating was a popular pastime *c*. 1900 and, more importantly, was a means of winter transportation on the lake. It is still a winter sport today but most often on the east branch, which is more shallow and freezes earlier. The large iceboats shown here in front of Gibson Landing were capable of considerable speed, probably the fastest these people had ever traveled. (Courtesy Doug Nichols.)

This 1920s photograph shows sailboats in front of the Keuka Yacht Club, which at that time was on the east side in Keuka Village. These A-scows, the pride of the club, are probably not racing, because the crews are of different sizes. The Wagener Mansion and the barns of the Lee farm to its right are visible on the horizon. The Garrett Chapel had not yet been built.

58

E-scows, the fastest sailboats in the yacht club's fleet, leave the Keuka Yacht Club in the 1950s. Judging from the ages of some of the crew, this is probably a class rather than a race.

Every Sunday and holiday during the summer, the Keuka Yacht Club, on the west side opposite the bluff, races three different classes of sailboats—Stars (shown here), Lightnings, and E-scows. The races are a thing of beauty and are interesting to watch, especially for those who sail.

At the Grove Springs Hotel, sailing draws hotel guests as spectators in this *c.* 1915 postcard. The Erie Railroad, which owned the trains and steamboats, offered this description of life at Keuka Lake in its promotional brochure: "Every one seems to be possessed with a desire to secure the greatest amount of comfort with the least expenditure of energy and the result is complete rest, delightful enjoyment, and perfect health."

Many rowboats line the beach at Central Point in this 1905 photograph from the Rapalee-Vosberg Collection. The posing of the two people standing in the boat, seemingly in conversation, is strange.

60

The building pictured above was constructed as a dance hall by A. Peris in 1932. It was later converted to a skating rink and a marina (below) owned by Rod Pierce. In March 1948, Keuka Motor and Marine Service, then owned by Frank Lanphear, burned, losing more than 100 boats in the showroom as well as storage from the old dance hall and skating rink. After the fire, Lanphear rebuilt the building and the business. Today it is known as Morgan Marine.

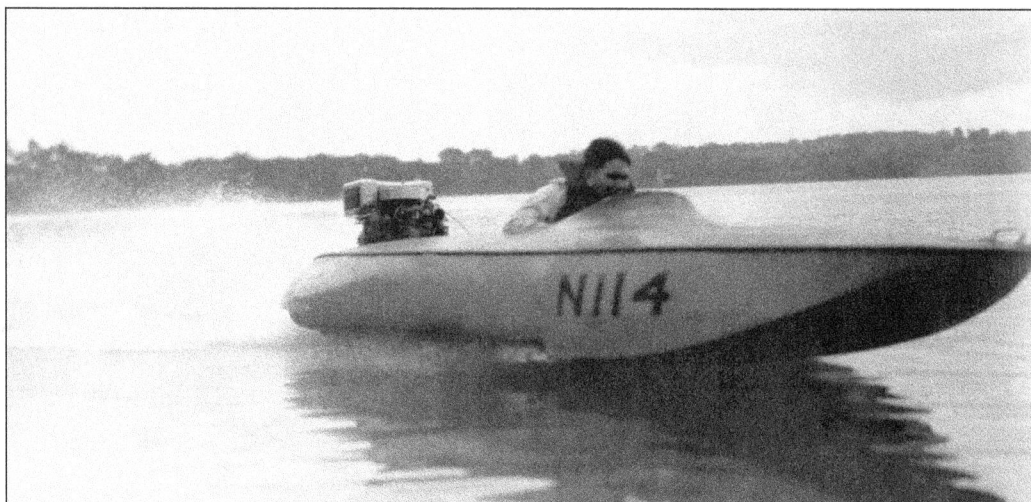

A boat like this was the dream of every boy on the lake. All that was needed to reach this dream was a small motor of 10 horsepower or less and a lightweight frame. It helped if it looked like a racing boat, for in a child's mind, the number on the side made the boat much faster. (Courtesy Candy Pierce.)

Penn Yan 24' Voyager Cabin, Model VIC
Length, c.l., 23'3" Beam 96" I/O hp to 160

Shown here is a press release photograph for the New York City National Motor Boat Show in January 1964. Penn Yan Boats Inc. expanded its line of fiberglass boats and continued the Wood Lapstrake line. This model is the 24-foot Voyager Cabin, model VIC. The company's boats were tested and photographed on Keuka Lake.

Does he look proud of that fish, or what? The chair in the boat reveals that he probably faced the stern and caught the fish on a Seth Green rig. One man, alone in a boat like this early in the morning, would put a meal on the table almost every time he went out.

The net rests in the oar lock, and the fisherman stands near the bow to show off the boat. Many boat enthusiasts looking at this photograph will see the boat and not the fish.

Ben Reno (left), a well-known boatbuilder working in Keuka Village, is pictured here with Dick Canfield. He and others in Keuka Village had as many as 70 boats available to rent. Today, his rowboats are highly prized for restoration; the Oliver House has one in its collection. (Courtesy Bob Canfield.)

Three

THE VILLAGES

The villages on Keuka Lake—Penn Yan, Hammondsport, Branchport, and Keuka Park—are connected by more than the use of the lake as their water source. They were all served by the same steamboat lines. In addition, the Penn Yan, Keuka Park, and Branchport Railway joined the three villages. The small towns all had similar commerce, including providing services to farmers.

Transportation around the lake began with sailboats, which were replaced by steamboats and supplemented by a canal and railroads. The canal that connected Keuka to Seneca Lake and the world was abandoned in the 1870s. Finally, paved roads and the automobile brought on the demise of both rail and steam. The railroad serving Hammondsport has since folded. One of the railroads serving Penn Yan did not return after the flood of 1972, and the other now terminates there.

The above drawing of the lake comes from a label for a pony basket, used for selling table grapes.

In 1897, construction began on a railway from Penn Yan to Branchport. The line started at the Great Northern Railroad depot on Jacob Street (now East Elm). A trolley car can be seen up the street not far from the station in this postcard view. In August 1897, when it made its inaugural run, the tracks were laid only as far as Electric Park.

When the Penn Yan, Keuka Park, and Branchport Railway passed through Penn Yan, it could travel only at the agreed 20 miles per hour so as not to scare the horses. Actually, the electric trolley was so quiet that the danger was only to pedestrians. On opening day, rides were free and people rode until late in the evening.

The "Pie, Cake, and Biscuit" line, as it was sometimes called, continued out of Penn Yan on Elm Street, with the tracks going down the middle of the street. Although the street is unpaved in this postcard view, it was later paved with bricks. In 1936, as a Work Projects Administration job, the tracks on Elm Street were removed.

Near the middle of the railway from Penn Yan to Branchport, an electric generating plant that was used to supply power for the trains was built. The area beside the plant on Brandy Bay was known as Electric Park. This print, made from a stereographic slide, shows the electric generating building and general offices. The building stands today as a private residence.

On any railroad, wrecks and fatalities were unfortunately common in the early 1900s. Car 15 was hit by car 10 at the carbarns in Electric Park. In the background is the dance pavilion, which was a popular destination on the railway in the summer. Special trains ran from Penn

Yan and Branchport for an evening at Electric Park. The steamboats also ran special excursions from landings on the east side to the docks at the park.

Using 100-man construction crews, between one quarter and one third of a mile of track was laid per day. Until the crews neared Branchport, the entire run was fairly level and made for fast track-laying. As a freight carrier, the railway was an immediate success.

The Penn Yan, Keuka Park, and Branchport Railway passed through Keuka Park in front of the college, where it turned west to go to Kinney's Corners. College students traveled into Penn Yan on the railway along with local residents. This 1920s scene shows the college stop. Note the sign on the front of the car advertising a Tom Mix movie at the Elmwood Theater in Penn Yan.

Car 11 stopped along its route for this postcard photograph. Despite the hard benches, passengers enjoyed the breezy open cars when they were used during the summer. By October 1897, the railway extended all the way to Branchport. This card is from the collection of the author's great-grandmother Emily Bogart Church, who probably rode on the Penn Yan, Keuka Park, and Branchport Railway.

Branchport was the terminus of the line. A connection to the steamboats existed there, although it was not direct as in Penn Yan or Hammondsport. No other railroad served Branchport.

Car 11 looks its age in this photograph from the early 1920s. Passenger service was discontinued in 1927, but freight continued on for a number of years. Partially visible behind the car is a passenger shelter.

In January 1902, fire destroyed the Branchport Hotel. Pictured in front of the hotel are, from left to right, owner George Swarts, Fred Lynn, Casper Hibbard, John Laird, Albert Lynn, Luther Jackson, and Jock Pierce (on the wagon). The boy on the porch is unidentified.

Dr. J.C. Wightman is shown in his rig in front of his stone house, which still stands today on the lake at the south edge of Branchport. He was a highly respected doctor who, as with many doctors at that time, would willingly go wherever and whenever needed.

Dr. Wightman befriended Asa Brown, who, as an orphan, was adopted by the Seneca Indians. Brown then revealed to him where the mother of Red Jacket was buried. Red Jacket was a noted orator and leader of the Senecas. He was recognized by his red jacket given to him by the British. His Seneca name was Sagoyewatha. The heirs of Dr. Wightman had this monument erected to mark the burial place. Verdi Burtch, noted Branchport ornithologist and naturalist, is shown at the monument in 1943, 10 years after it was erected.

In the background of this A.R. Stone photograph, the *Springstead*, named for boatbuilder A.W. Springstead, has its coal unloaded. The steam-powered barge, used both as a freight carrier and tow boat, worked on the lake for years until it sunk near Hammondsport.

The pinnacle to the east of Branchport was used by many photographers to get a bird's-eye view of the village. This photograph predates the construction of the railway in 1897. The Methodist church appears on the right, and next to it the Presbyterian church, which burned in 1912. The Baptist church is to the west of the four corners. In the middle of the scene, Guyanoga Creek feeds into Keuka Lake. The docks can be seen on the extreme left.

Highway construction was much slower in the 1920s. Other than the cement mixer, a crane, and trucks, most of the work was done by hand. Before the construction reached Hammondsport, many streams had to be bridged and countless tons of shale removed to make a level roadway.

When the state built the highway that is now designated 54A, batch boxes of dry components were brought to Branchport on the Penn Yan, Keuka Park, and Branchport Railway and transported to the site by Model T trucks. This 1924 photograph was taken in front of the Campbell's Beach driveway.

The Branchport Universalist Church was built in 1852 on Main Street south of the four corners. The congregation kept shrinking until the church finally dissolved. In 1920, the building was razed. The lumber was used to construct a house directly across the street, near St. Luke's.

Built in 1880, the Methodist church in Branchport was the second building for that congregation, which was organized in 1866. The first church burned, and the neighboring Presbyterian church was used while this building was being built.

St. Luke's Episcopal Church on Main Street in Branchport has been a very active congregation since the church was organized in 1863. The building was erected in 1866. Built of native stone, the exterior is virtually unchanged today.

Near Branchport is the Friend House, the last home of Jemima Wilkinson, the Universal Friend. The Friend, a religious mystic, and her followers from Rhode Island were the first group of white pioneers to settle in the area of what is now Yates County. Their first site was on the west side of Seneca Lake. After the pioneers had built her a dwelling, she joined them. Her final home, shown here, was built for her by her disciples in the town of Jerusalem. It stands today as a private residence on Friend Road.

This aerial photograph of the north end of Keuka Lake's east branch shows most of Penn Yan and the area to the south. The oval in the left center beside Route 54 is the racetrack at the old Yates County Fairgrounds. In the late 1950s, the fairgrounds were moved to their current location outside the village. The Lake Street Plaza now occupies the original site.

The circus coming to town was always a big occasion. The performers usually paraded from the train to Main Street and on to the fairgrounds. The parade, used to entice everyone to come to the circus, gave townspeople a look at the animals, the clowns, and the other acts. This 1905 panoramic photograph, taken in front of the Oliver House, shows the parade moving down Main Street.

A circus tent at the old fairgrounds on Lake Street is the subject of this photograph made from the original glass plate from the Rapalee-Vosberg Collection. While this may not be the same circus as the one parading in the photograph on page 78, it could be.

Penn Yan was the summer home of the James M. Cole Circus. Young Jimmy Cole, billed as "America's Youngest Elephant Trainer," was 13 at the time of this early-1950s publicity photograph. Penn Yan always showed pride in its association with the Cole Circus.

The Fallbrook Railroad, later part of the New York Central system, ran along the Keuka Lake outlet to the industries east of the Main Street Bridge. Shown here is the extension that ran to the businesses on the west side of the bridge all the way to the lake. These businesses include the ice harvesting at the lake and the boat docks. Prior to the abandonment of the Crooked Lake Canal in the 1870s, the area behind the track workers was the canal towpath.

In the late 19th century, many industries populated the Keuka Lake outlet in Penn Yan. This photograph was made from the original glass plate of the H. and E.D. Tuthill Malt House on Water Street. The business, served by barges on the water side and a railroad spur on the east, shipped malt to the major cities in the East. Note the private yacht tied alongside.

This photograph, also from a glass plate, shows the New York Central depot in Penn Yan, another malt house, and the T.S. Burns cold storage building, which burned in 1897. The railroad bed was built in the place of either the abandoned Crooked Lake Canal or its towpath. The Keuka Lake outlet is in the foreground.

The Birkett Mills wagon is shown on the Main Street Bridge, between the Andrews Mill and its own mill on the left. The first mill in Penn Yan was established in this location in 1797. Note that the unpaved street bears cobblestones to help provide a firm surface.

Main Street in Penn Yan is not yet paved, but utility poles and wires are visible. The Great Atlantic & Pacific Tea Company (A & P) occupies the store under the awning. Signs on the front portico of Struble's Arcade advertise the telegraph office, the *Penn Yan Democrat*, and Biret the photographer. Biret specialized in portraiture; some examples of his fine work appear in local collections.

"Number, please," says the operator. The Penn Yan Telephone Company planned to have 500 subscribers before July 1, 1903. The *Penn Yan Chronicle* account does not say if the company reached that goal, but it did place 125 poles in the village and 75 along the lake at that time.

The trolley tracks remain visible in this Depression-era photograph of Penn Yan's four corners. *Billy the Kid* was playing at the Elmwood. The number of people and cars on the downtown streets gives the appearance that some special activity is taking place. The reason for the tables along the curb is unknown.

This four corners view in the opposite direction looks up East Elm Street toward the railroad tracks. The ladies crossing the street against the light are jay-walking; some things never change. Unfortunately, one thing that did change was the streetlights. In the 1990s, lights like the one just to the right of the traffic light were installed. A U-turn around that traffic light would be a tight maneuver.

W.H. Whitfield and Son body builders (bus bodies, that is) was a long-established business in Penn Yan. Photographs for company records were often taken on Main Street, in this case in front of the Fox home. Its successor, Coach and Equipment, is one of Penn Yan's major employers.

The Adams Express Company horse-drawn wagon is shown in 1898. The wagon hauled freight locally and transferred goods between the steamboats and the railroads. With all the industry around Penn Yan at that time, it was probably kept quite busy.

Owner Rod Pierce displays the Pierce Freight Lines trucks on East Elm Street in the late 1930s. He formerly owned Pierce Marine; the writing is still visible on the door of the truck on the right. In the right background, beside the tracks, is the spout to fill the steam engines with water. (Courtesy Candy Pierce.)

Penn Yan Express trucks carried the Penn Yan name all over the country, as did Penn Yan Boats; both are gone. President Robert L. Hinson, the taller man standing beside one of the company's tandem trailers, was always very proud of his trucks, his terminal, and his employees. In the late 1970s, some controversy arose when he (successfully) sought permission for the tandems to travel from the Penn Yan terminal to the expressway at Bath and to the New York State Thruway.

The Liberty Street Bridge in this *c.* 1900 postcard is considerably smaller than the span there today, which carries two state routes. The bridge crossed over the Keuka outlet and the railroad tracks that went out to the head of the lake. The scene at the top of page 80 would have been to the right of this photograph.

St. Mark's Episcopal Church, at the corner of Main and Clinton Streets in Penn Yan, was built in 1879 at a cost of $9,000. The exterior consists of pressed brick with black mortar on a stone foundation. This photograph was made from a glass plate from the Rapalee-Vosberg Collection.

Bordwell's Drug Store was one of the "anchor" stores at the four corners in Penn Yan, visible in the photograph below, to the right of the pole in the center. After many years at this location, the store moved to the new Lake Street Plaza. An office building now occupies this corner.

Main Street in downtown Penn Yan is shown here on a snowy winter morning. Today, we haul the snow away to clear the streets, but in this c. 1910 photograph, the snow remained until it melted. The view appears to have been taken in front of Lown's Department Store.

87

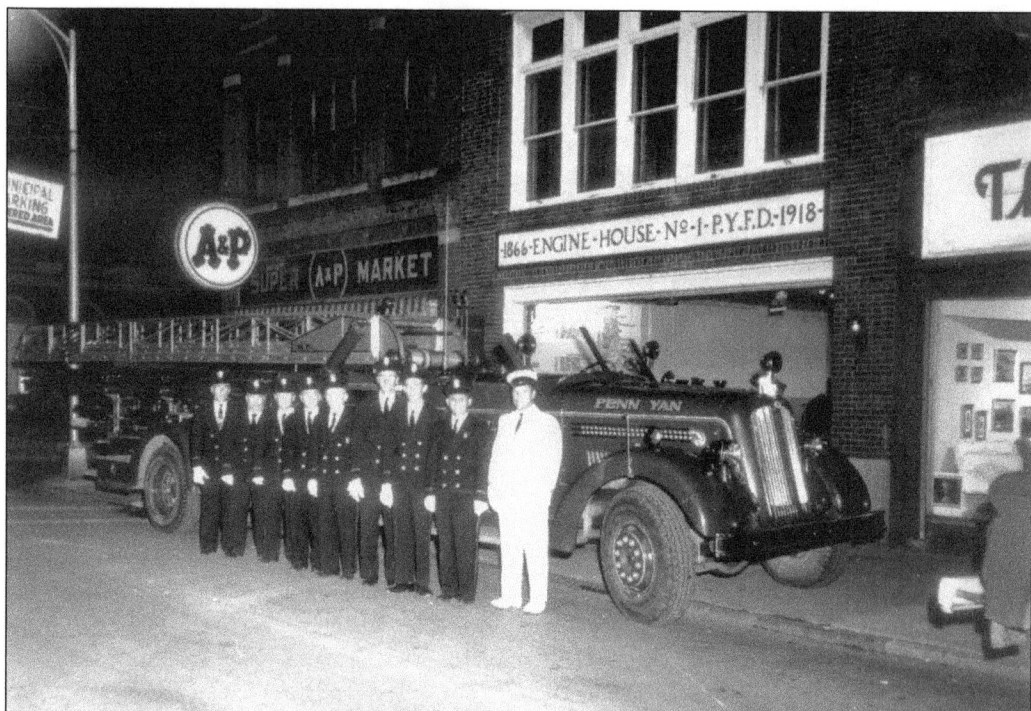

Penn Yan has the dubious distinction of its firehouse burning with all the trucks inside. This evening photograph was taken prior to that disastrous Main Street fire in 1968. The Penn Yan Fire Department is now as well equipped as any department in the state.

During World War II, the monthly draft call was usually photographed after induction in front of the Benham Hotel in Penn Yan. After the picture, the men boarded their bus for transport to the basic training base. On October 19, 1942, these 73 men leave for training, all much younger than the men in the groups two years later would be.

The Penn Yan Academy opened for classes in 1859. Population was growing rapidly at the time, and it was soon necessary to build two elementary schools. Children of farmers living outside the village often boarded in town during the school term in order to receive an education that was not usually offered in the country.

At the Apple Blossom Festival, the Apple Blossom Queen and her court prepare for the annual parade. The carriage in which they are riding once belonged to Jemima Wilkinson, the Universal Friend. The undercarriage was built in Philadelphia in the late 1700s, and the coach was built in Canandaigua in 1811. This was the last public use of the carriage, which is now housed in the Granger Homestead Carriage Museum in Canandaigua.

Many photographs of the Hammondsport harbor were taken from this vantage point on Bully Hill between 1885 and 1910 for postcards. Most of the village can be seen, especially the waterfront, the hub of all the action at that time.

This 1905 postcard shows the railroad and the steamboat docks together at the end of the lake. The depot is still there today, although the Bath and Hammondsport Railroad is not. Part of the *Penn Yan*, white stripes on the stack, is visible over the steamboat landing shelter.

This postcard photograph shows the *Mary Bell* at the Hammondsport docks, with Water Street on the right. The rail spur in the left foreground leads to the Lyon Brothers grape-packing warehouse. The lady walking near the tracks will get the skirts of her white dress muddy, which was not uncommon with unpaved streets.

In the period from 1910 through 1915, the Keuka Lake waterfront in Hammondsport was even busier than in prior times, with the advent of Glenn Curtiss. The seaplane was developed here in Champlin Beach, which is now a public swimming area and where the *Keuka Maid* is docked.

The Hammondsport Presbyterian Church, built in 1847, is in the square facing north. Note the absence of any poles or wires. The steeple in this *c.* 1890 photograph was destroyed but has since been replaced.

Hammondsport native son Glenn Curtiss invented the seaplane on Keuka Lake and flew often, to the delight of the local residents. Here, a considerable gathering of spectators along the shore examines the HS flying boat and hopes to get rides *c.* 1912. Due to the size of the crowd, all dressed in their Sunday best, it must have been a preannounced flight, which was Curtiss's habit.

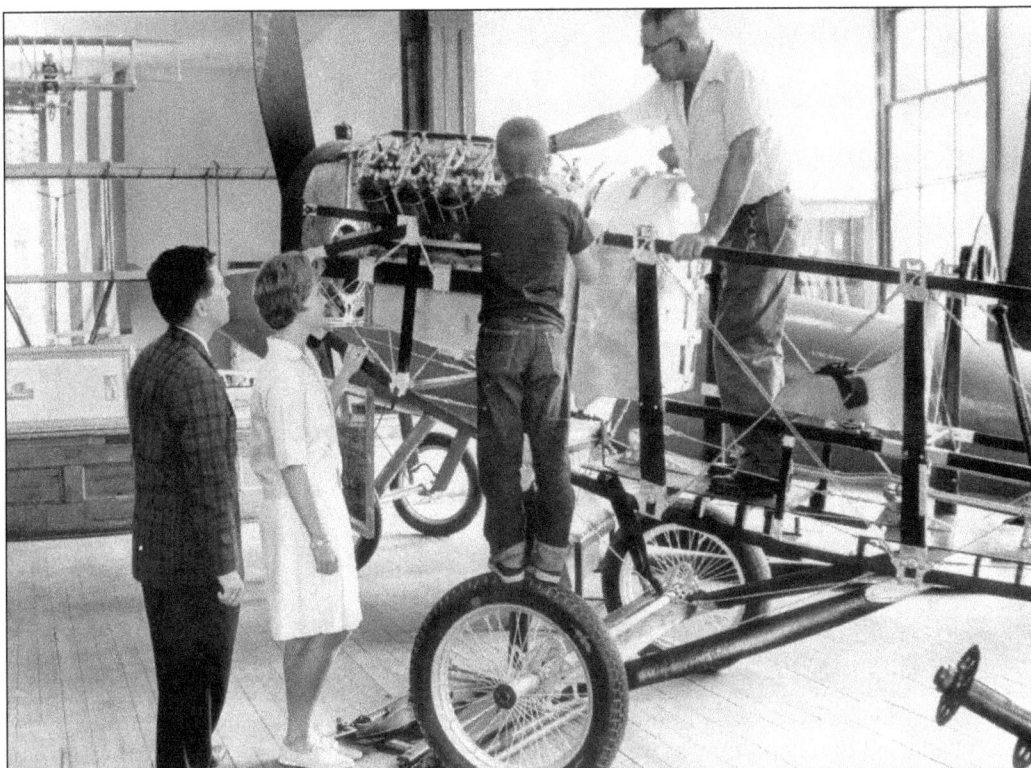

Otto Kohl, founder of the Glenn H. Curtiss Museum of Local History, shows the OX-5 engine in a stripped-down Jenny to a young future aviator. The museum was originally housed in the old Hammondsport Main Street School, which now functions as offices of the Town of Urbana and the Hammondsport Village Library.

The Keuka Lake Art Association held its 1975 show in the park in Hammondsport. That tradition continues today as an annual art show weekend. Other weekends host arts and crafts shows, concerts in the park, Christmas in the park, and other events.

This postcard view to the west from Keuka College's Ball Hall was taken before the Penn Yan, Keuka Park, and Branchport tracks were laid in 1897. This view shows the opposite direction of the one at the top of page 96. The street locations are about the only thing unchanged.

Keuka College in May 1897 consisted of one building—Ball Hall, shown here in a view from the south. Ball Hall, now well over 100 years old, is being replaced with a new building that re-creates, in a contemporary form, the original building using architecture present in Ball Hall and other campus buildings. The old Ball Hall will then be demolished.

94

The Norton Chapel in the Jephson Center for Christian Education was named in honor of Arthur H. Norton, college president from 1919 to 1935, and Lucretia Davis Jephson, friend and benefactor of youth. The nondenominational chapel was dedicated in October 1964. Its design is modern, with exposed beams and high ceilings.

This 1950s aerial view shows the campus from the west. The water tower on the left was removed in the 1970s, and Norton Chapel had not yet been built. Most of the additions to the campus since this photograph—the gymnasium, student center, and dorms—would be to the south (right), outside this view. Unfortunately, the large elm trees are gone.

The Keuka College campus remains a place of beauty in the winter. This view was taken from the east of Ball Hall, looking south. The building in the background, Harrington Hall, as well as Hegeman Hall, have been extensively remodeled and almost appear to be new constructions.

96

Four

THE VINES

Grapes have been grown around Keuka Lake since the 1850s, when the Reverend Bostwick planted some in Hammondsport. Grapes thrived in the growing conditions and soil around the lake. Other people soon took notice and also planted grapes. Keuka Lake table grapes soon became recognized as quality fruit. Many grape-packing houses appeared around the lake and provided a major portion of the freight on the steamships and railroads.

In 1861, the Pleasant Valley Wine Company was licensed as New York Bonded Winery No. 1, a distinction it still holds. Over the years until Prohibition, a number of wineries opened: Taylor, Germania, Urbana, McCorn, and Gold Seal, among others. Taylor, Gold Seal, Great Western, and Pleasant Valley survived Prohibition. Through various corporate mergers and purchases, these wineries no longer exist or are part of Canandaigua Brands.

The closing of the large wineries in the 1970s and 1980s depressed the grape industry around Keuka Lake until the passage of the Farm Wine Bill by the New York legislature in 1976. This allowed the operation of a "farm" winery and the annual production of 150,000 gallons of wine. Today, the Finger Lakes region boasts nearly 60 wineries that are producing some world-class wines. Keuka Lake can claim 10 of these. Much of the credit goes to the late Dr. Konstantin Frank, who demonstrated that European grapes could be grown in the cold climate of New York's Finger Lakes. Founded by him, Vinifera Wine Cellars is considered by many to be the premier New York winery.

The end of the bluff, as shown in this 1890 photograph from a glass plate, was heavily planted in grapes. The Wagener Mansion and the future site of the Garrett Chapel are situated to the right, outside the image. One of the requirements of a vineyard is that it be well drained. Consequently, the vines were planted up and down the hill, a practice that was only later determined to cause topsoil to be washed into the lake.

This image was reproduced from a lantern slide used by the New York State Education Department in 1921. The slide was hand-colored and labeled as having been taken on the bluff, looking east.

The steep hillsides on the bluff were better suited to hand-tended vineyards than to other crops needing mechanization. Today, most vineyards are on less steep land, although most are still within sight of the water to reap the benefits of the lake's microclimate. This view looks east from the bluff across the east branch of Keuka Lake.

This view looks south from Esperanza Road down the west branch. The house visible in the left foreground is the Chestnuts. Esperanza is hidden by the trees in the right foreground. The southernmost point on the west side of the lake is approximately across from the end of the bluff.

This original postcard print, "Picking Lake Keuka Grapes," was hand-tinted with very soft, muted colors. Picking was a chore that women and older men usually were given. The only lifting involved was hauling the boxes to the end of the rows. Pickers were paid for the number of boxes filled, not the hours worked.

"Picking Grapes at Hammondsport, NY" is the title of this postcard produced by photographer and vineyardist Harry M. Benner. He has made the scene look romantic—hardly the reaction of anyone who has picked grapes.

The pressing room of the Empire State Wine Company in Penn Yan can be seen in this postcard by Harris. The walls in the stone winery were between one and two feet thick. The building could not be modified for use and was razed in the 1990s.

·LAKE KEUKA GRAPES·

PACKED BY

This colorful label was used by grape packers who did not have their own label. On the back is printed, "Guile & Windnagle, of Penn Yan, NY, Manufacture Baskets of all kinds and they make a Specialty of Fruit Packages and Picking Boxes. See their stock and get prices."

The McMath and Morgan Fruit House was a fruit-packing warehouse located off East Elm Street in Penn Yan, close to the Great Northern Railroad tracks. This Harris photograph, taken *c.* 1895, shows that the packing crew is mostly women. Housewives could earn extra money at this seasonal work and were most likely better at it.

Samuel McMath was a packer and shipper of table grapes, sent by railroad to the cities of the Northeast. He also had an interest in the steamboat lines, so he was dependent on the grape crop for much of his income.

The Whitfield Peerless Grape Wagon, made in Penn Yan, is loaded with pony baskets of grapes ready to be transferred to a refrigerated rail car. Unfortunately, because the labels on the baskets cannot be seen, we do not know if the wagon carries any of the labels shown here.

Andrew Mackay created Royal Brand for the grapes he packed and shipped. He was a local grocer but also packed fruit for shipment. These colorful labels made a very attractive package.

103

The crew poses in this Keuka Village grape-packing warehouse. Photographer W.J. Harris had the ladies over-pack the baskets; the workers normally would not have filled them this full. The covers, with the labels already attached, are in front of the baskets. (Courtesy Tom Packard.)

The D.W. Putnam Company had a grape-packing warehouse on the lakefront in Hammondsport. The company, organized in the 1920s, expanded into wine and champagne with the coming of repeal. This c. 1930 photograph shows the packing crew. (Courtesy Tom Packard.)

Pony baskets and picking boxes were manufactured locally. This print illustrates the George W. Finton sawmill and grape box manufactory on Keuka Lake at Finton's Landing. The vineyards and outbuilding are gone, but the house is there, now operating as the Finton's Landing Bed and Breakfast.

This long, narrow building at the docks in Penn Yan was used for the trans-loading of grapes from the steamboats to the refrigerated rail cars. It was also used to move freight in the other direction, but grapes were the main cargo. These dollies are loaded with pony baskets.

The Keuka Lake Ice Company runway carried ice cut from the lake to its ice-storage building on West Lake Road. The icehouse, with a capacity of 25,000 tons, burned in 1916. Note the smokestack of the Penn Yan Municipal Water Plant in the background. The cottage in the foreground is named Nikko.

The ice ramp extended out into the lake alongside the entrance to the Keuka Lake outlet. The ice was harvested, usually around the first of February, for about a week. Some was shipped out on the railroad; the balance was stored for the grape-shipping season in the fall.

These two photographs made from glass plates show the ice being harvested from the lake. The men would use saws to cut the ice into blocks, which were then loaded on the sleighs. The horses would haul the blocks to the rail cars for shipment on the New York Central or to the storage buildings, which were insulated with sawdust to hold the ice through the hot summer. Ice was also sold locally to use in iceboxes.

The Guile and Windnagle Company used the logs in the foreground to manufacture all kinds of baskets, including pony baskets for grapes. The company's stone building was located on the outlet. Baskets were made here from 1891 until 1945. The building burned in 1947 in a spectacular fire observed by hundreds.

The Yates Lumber and Basket Company was one of many basket factories in the Keuka Lake area c. 1900. Most of them manufactured pony baskets, but grape-picking boxes and bushel baskets were also made for the local packers.

This "Choice Lake Keuka Grapes" generic label was printed by the *Yates County Chronicle* in Penn Yan. Smaller packers who could not afford their own labels had to add their name and variety. In the 19th and early 20th centuries, most newspapers also did printing jobs to keep their presses busy between editions.

The trains on the Fallbrook Line of the New York Central pulled up along the dock at Penn Yan to load grapes brought by the steamboats, as in the photograph at the top of the next page or the one at the bottom of page 105. This photograph was printed from half of an 8- by 10-inch glass plate. The building with the "Fruit House" sign is still there.

This postcard is titled "Shipping Fruit from W.N. Wise Wharf, Penn Yan, NY." William N. Wise was an entrepreneur; he was a partner in Hollowell and Wise Hardware on Main Street and had an interest in one of the steamship lines.

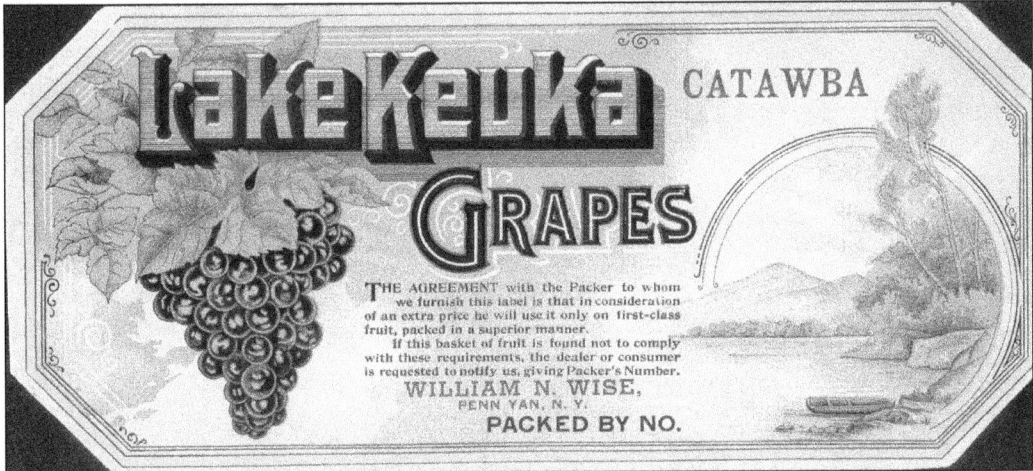

William N. Wise was also a grape packer. A civic-minded citizen, he was instrumental in raising funds to build the Soldiers and Sailors Memorial Hospital in Penn Yan. In the mid-1920s, he gave a silver spoon to every baby born in the hospital.

This beautiful *c.* 1900 photograph shows the view across the northern end of Keuka Lake on a calm, quiet day. The Empire State Winery is located in the large building to the right of center. In the center sits an ice-storage warehouse. The Keuka Lake outlet is in front of the icehouse.

Taken by the same photographer as the one above, this view shows the Empire State Winery from its vineyards to the east. Today the photographer's vantage point is all homes. The area to the left of center is a Penn Yan village park named after Red Jacket.

Many of the Empire State Wine Company's products were sold under the State Seal brand name. This photograph shows the staff in the packing room, although from the way it is decorated one would think it was a tasting room.

The Empire State Winery cellars contained many of these casks for aging wine. The man in the white lab coat appears to be taking samples from the 50-gallon barrels, also used for aging.

This photograph of a section of the Empire State Wine Company vineyards along the lake south of Penn Yan shows grape baskets being loaded on a wagon. They will be taken to the winery to be pressed. The ladies picking are dressed quite well for a day's work; they obviously

knew the photographer was coming. Note the barrels stored in the vineyard. Either they are waiting to be cleaned, or they are beyond their useful lives.

This couple on a picnic toasts with State Seal champagne. If the Empire State Wine Company were still in business, it would not call its sparkling wines "champagne" but would say they had been made by "methode champagnoise." That the Finger Lakes wine industry observes these conventions is a sign of maturity.

The White Top Winery on Keuka's west side was the only winery whose sole product was champagne. The people in the foreground are probably walking to the winery from Gibson's Landing just to the north. The building is used for boat storage today.

The Urbana Winery was later known for its Gold Seal brand. Winemaker Charles Fournier, working with Dr. Konstantin Frank, was a leader in introducing vinifera and French-American hybrid grapes into production in the Finger Lakes.

This White House Wine Cellar image was prepared for a prospectus to attract investors to a new winery. Why the winery did not go into business is unknown. Like most of the wineries in existence at the start of the 20th century, it most likely would not have survived Prohibition.

"Germania Wine Cellars, Hammondsport, NY, Champagne Vaults" is the title of this postcard view. The bottles of champagne are shown in riddling racks, where they are gently turned daily to work the sediment from fermentation into the neck; the sediment is removed before final corking.

The tasting area at Gold Seal was one of the most pleasant places to end a tour—overlooking the lake. Knowledgeable locals would attempt to take the last tour of the day, which would not be pressured to move from the tasting deck by a following tour.

The champagne cellars at Gold Seal were dug back into the hill, deep in the winery. These bottles, being aged, have completed the process except for labeling, unlike the bottles in the opposite photograph.

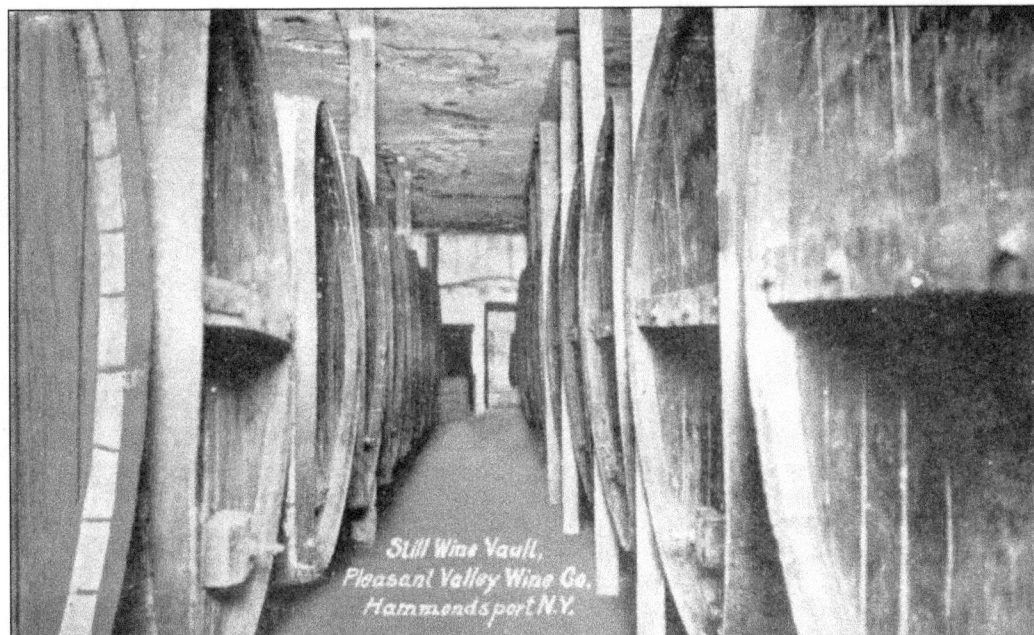

Still Wine Vault, Pleasant Valley Wine Co, Hammondsport N.Y.

These casks, stored in cellars dug into the hillsides, contain Pleasant Valley wines. Aging the wines in oak casks (usually barrels today) is a method still used to impart an oak flavor, adding to the complexity of the wine.

Any aerial views of Keuka Lake will show some vineyards and probably a winery. In this *c.* 1950 photograph, Gold Seal is in the foreground, with its vineyards behind, and Taylor Vineyards is in the center. Today, the Heron Hill Winery is located in the area near the right center of this

image, Bully Hill to the far left horizon, and Walter Taylor's home on the horizon in the center. Unfortunately, the Gold Seal buildings are no longer used as a winery.

Linda Jackson, performing winter work, ties grapes in her vineyard on East Lake Road. From the look of the ice on the lake, it is early spring, and the ice has started to break. Keuka College is visible on the shore opposite.

A group of tourists at the Great Western Winery in Hammondsport in the 1970s is shown white oak casks and hears an explanation of how table wines are made. Wineries then and the farm wineries today see education as part of their marketing.

The vineyards of the Finger Lakes region produce much of the premium wine grapes grown in New York. The grapes shown here have been picked by a mechanical picker and will be trucked to one of the wineries for pressing. (Courtesy Ed Webber.)

The Taylor and Great Western Wineries no longer use these facilities, which were originally built as the Columbia Wine Company in the 1860s. The Taylor Wine Company was one of the wineries that managed to survive Prohibition by making sacramental wines. Other wineries stayed in business selling juice to individuals, along with very specific instructions of what not to do or the juice might turn into wine.

The entrance to the Taylor Wine Company in Hammondsport fits about anyone's perception of what a winery should look like. Founded in 1880, Taylor was the largest producer of premium champagnes in the country and had the distinction of being the largest wine producer in the East. (Courtesy Ed Webber.)

This pressing crew receives partially crushed grapes from the floor above. At this point, the bunches have been de-stemmed and the skins broken to release the juice. They are put into a press that will exert tremendous hydraulic pressure to extract all the juice possible.

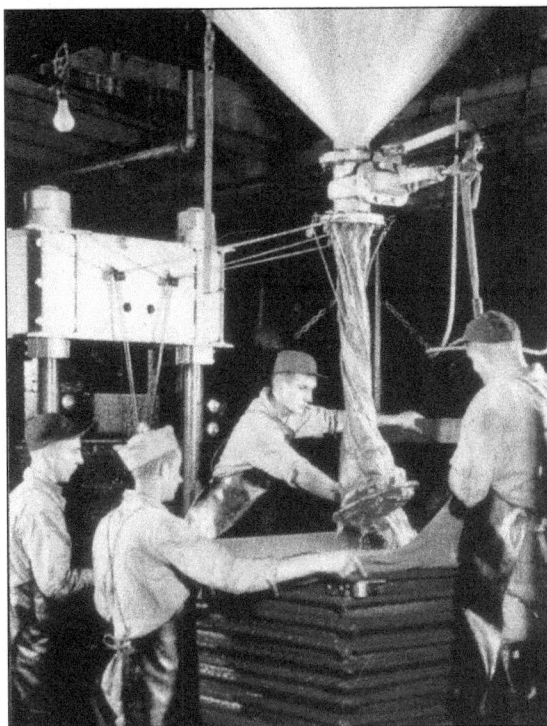

Greyton H. Taylor and his son Walter (front) pose with a tote of grapes being moved from the truck to the pressing area by towmotor. Walter, who just recently died, left Taylor and founded the Bully Hill Vineyards in 1970, one of the most successful small wineries in the Finger Lakes.

125

The farm at the Hunt Country Vineyards, operated by Art and Joyce Hunt, is a "Century Farm"—they are the sixth generation to till the soil there. In this *c.* 1890 photograph of their house, Art's grandfather Floyd is the boy sitting on the steps at the left.

The Heron Hill Winery has been completely remodeled such that it is difficult today to find the original building (above). Releasing their first vintage in 1977, John and Josephine Ingle have long had a reputation for hospitality and fine wines.

126

Like many small wineries, the Keuka Overlook was a second career for both Bob and Terry Barrett. They left their jobs in Cleveland to start it in 1994. The winery is located in a renovated barn across the road from their restored Victorian farmhouse bed and breakfast, overlooking Keuka Lake.

Mechanical harvesting of commercial grapes began in the Finger Lakes in the late 1960s. Today in the Keuka Lake area, 90 percent of the grapes are harvested this way. The pickers, tall enough to straddle the vines, appear very awkward when seen on the road. (Courtesy Ed Webber.)

Another perfect day ends on Keuka Lake. (Courtesy Dan Mitchell.)

www.ingramcontent.com/pod-product-compliance
Lightning Source LLC
Chambersburg PA
CBHW050642110426
42813CB00007B/1892